to the Doctors Mesarov

with the best wishes of

Aaron Bohrod

WISCONSIN SKETCHES

BOHROD   GARD   LEFEBVRE

Bohrod

Aaron Bohrod

WISC ONSIN SKETCHES

DRAWINGS by AARON BOHROD

WORDS by ROBERT E. GARD

EDITED by MARK E. LEFEBVRE

First Edition
ISBN 0-88361-026-4
Library of Congress Card Number 73-89027

Printed in the United States of America for
Wisconsin House, Ltd. by Straus Printing
and Publishing Co., Inc., Madison, Wisconsin

WISCONSIN HOUSE, LTD.
BOOK PUBLISHERS
P.O. Box 2118·Madison, Wis. 53701

Most of the drawings reproduced in this book are from the period 1948 to about 1954: from the time I arrived in Wisconsin to become artist-in-residence at the University to a moment when the demands of a long-term intensive still life vein of painting precluded extended state-wide wanderings and exhaustive sketchbook jottings. These are selections from Wisconsin-oriented material, some of which served as the sketch basis for more comprehensive works in oil and in gouache. Others are drawings and designs done simply for the sheer love of drawing and the general celebration of life.

Bob Gard's poetic vision of Wisconsin and my own view of the state are separate and independent strains. Where these strains have touched and run together, our editor Mark Lefebvre has placed our work in contiguity. But this is not an "illustrated book" in the sense that the artist attempts to expand graphically on the written thought; nor has the writer worked around the visual material with words to similar purpose.

A good deal of the writing and drawing in this book lacks connective tissue. Each medium may be devoid of counterpart in the complimentary discipline. But the fact that there are so many points of thematic connection is a fortuitous circumstance that stems, perhaps, from the common interest in a setting and in a climate where we both have found aesthetic nourishment.

Aaron Bohrod

The words for this book are written out of a depth of love for Wisconsin earth and sky and people. They are not meant, nor do they pretend to be, poems to stand in their own right. They are expressions of simple sensibilities, of days among the seasons, of settings in awareness, of often only half-formed and hardly spoken impressions. They are of myself and represent a bond, a trust, and a belief in a state and of man. The words are written for people and reflect my appreciation of people and of my feeling for them and for the places in which they exist.

The words are a kind of testament, too, to the thing my friend Bohrod and I have tried to live for: the continuation of a spirit of unique relationship between creative man and nature and ideas as they have grown from the peculiar soil that was and is Wisconsin.

Our lives have been blessed with careers devoted to man's expressiveness; and so the sketches in words and pictures are intended to be intensely real, also personal, also universal.

This work is conceived expression of faith and affinity. I trust that, in a way, words and sketches, while not perfectly related, are inseparable; they are meant to fall into that relationship, and are dedicated to the concept of art and people.

Bohrod, the artist, twenty-five years artist-in-residence, continuer of a brave and noble art tradition that began with John Steuart Curry in 1936, and that continues to this day.

Gard, encourager of writers, of actors and of communities in search of a richer life through native arts.

Both Bohrod and I are devoted to a grassroots concept of art. He retired this year and his studio on the campus is lonely without him. I will continue on yet awhile, but the spirit of a state we have loved will not diminish now. It has been firmly established by the complex of the people who would possess, despite meager means, often, the leading soil in the nation to nurture a deep sensitiveness to nature and to an understanding of the meaning of art for all.

Robert E. Gard

This sketchbook is a book of life, the life each of us is living. I have arranged the drawings and words loosely, yet suggestively, to create different ways of seeing.

Mark E. Lefebvre

for Ruth and for Maryo

A windmill on a far farm hill

Will turn and turn against the force

That nature provides

In place of steam or electricity

To those who have vision

To erect a windmill on a hill,

And take advantage of the way the wind comes

Across the valley, lifting up the slope,

To strike the blades in air, petaled to receive

And turn and turn above the pasture well.

For me windmills are life.   They stand like neglected skeletons,

not many now are left . . . a few on hill, in barnyard, and pasture.

Mostly their blades are still, yet to me the silent blades turn

on in memory against the wind:

An entire rotation of man and of earth.

I have been restless,

And have wandered far from my home.

Into the heart of America I have moved

From town to town and place

To farm place.

I the eternal worker with earth.

I have understood how the earth-heart beats.

I have taken when young

Dusty steps behind the long harrow;

Or have held tearing bright cultivator shovels,

Pushing moist earth against the young corn.

I have thrust the shovels of the corn plow

Into the dark earth,

And have known the flow of steel-cut earth

Upon my feet.

I have seen the vining flowers

Open in the morning, turned toward sun,

The stem spiralled around barbed wire,

Or climbing taller corn stalks at the field's edge.

I have seen the road

Going away between hills,

And the square temple-tower

Of the grain elevator at the end.

I have been into the heart of America,

Have seen the people in trouble

In a time of trouble.

And who else here

Is a wanderer, and has seen

As I have seen, or felt

As I have felt?

I heard a pioneer cry:

Here oh heart of America

Where prairie ships sail,

Here oh heart

Is where my journey has blown me,

Here is the beginning of my life

For out of you

Is made the heart of the world.

Oh how to tell of Wisconsin,

She hued golden in fall and delicate in spring,

And I riding through her heart.

Watching waiting to hear from her,

Myself a sounding instrument

Giving back words for air, cloud, wood, and white water;

Words marking my passage.

I have seen her, yes, since I was a young man.

Watching her changes,

Feeling her tempos, her peoples,

And I have seen her nations assembled,

Studied the map of her nationalities spread broadside:

The slipping past in time and memory,

A spectacle of old churches, forgotten cabins,

And foreign names attached to small places.

I have watched her more recent arrivals gathered in Milwaukee,

Under high beams in a great hall,

Stricken into moving pools of color

By immense shafts of vibrating light:

Huge arcs humming from the beams,

Their colorwheel patterns falling in and among

The nimble dancers from many nations.

And I swept by my memory

Of strong earlier folk from foreign lands

Coming to us by sail, by steamer,

Slower wagon, and on foot, sweeping out

From eastern coasts, hastening to the heartlands.

Oh my heart, pause, let me feel,

Freed from your pulsing beat,

That pains to music and dancing feet.

Let me savor in silence the power of the folk.

Look now at the dancers on the wide floor:

Greeks, Serbs, and Croatians;

Germans, Norwegians;

Swiss, Lithuanians, Finns;

Russians, Irish, Poles;

Bavarians, Ukranians, Israeli;

Latvians, and Spaniards,

Blacks:

All, even as I,

For their power is in me transferred.

No native son, I, a visitor;

But exposed early to a power of thought,

That raced through time and left

A newer thrilling impress on America;

To give an insight to the soul of freedom,

And the better life. Man restless,

And great minds fermenting expansive ideas

That had source in progressive struggles

And star-aspiring ideals.

I have sought through man and season,

Traveled a thousand roads,

Sensed the sweep of time that drew her

through generations of builders

Toiling with forest, plow, steamboat, rail,

And now to forest-free farmlands and cutovers

Already growing toward a century of new pine.

Change, change from crossroads places,

Not so unpopulous a century ago,

To forgotten names or home places

From which the young folks can hardly wait

To flee to the city.

I have seen and noted the struggle,

Watched small cheese factories

And small town breweries disappear,

And big business come to the family farm.

Yet the change is no change,

For the spirit that drew me here,

As one of many who sensed that Wisconsin was different,

Remains. I know, for I have heard

The spirit calling me in woods: truly

The same voiceless thrill the Maine men felt,

And the New Hampshire men, and the Yorkers,

When they sought new land on prairie and among oak openings;

And themselves created, built, dreamed, suffered, and died;

For their bones lie in many small burial grounds.

I have found them, stones slanted against time,

On hilltops, and in weedy roadside meadows.

And I understand that here lay those who brought dreams

And made the first impress on the land.

Dam at Janesville

What nailers and spike-drivers these earlier heroes.
New rails through uncut forests and along rivers;
Canal diggers—Irishmen, Dutchmen, and English potters—
Spade, pick and shovel, among roots.
Seven foot deep for the larger steamboats.

I know a farmer at Endeavor whose grandfather
Turned the first spadeful for the canal at Portage.
He a potter by trade from Staffordshire,
Worked, plodded, heaved, fourteen-hour shifts,
That sternwheelers might roil water
And boil sand from Green Bay to New Orleans.

And these workers or others of the same driving breed,
Went into the northwoods to hack white pine;
Skid the logs out to the streams, first log
Six feet at the base, sometimes,
Second log not much less,
And the landlookers forever scanning out
Billions more board feet for tireless sawyers and axemen.

In the towns—Rhinelander, Stevens Point,
Wausau, Eau Claire, Menominie, and Oshkosh—
Dwelt the lordly barons of the woods.
There stand yet castles built by gold from white Wisconsin pine.
I pass them in awe for these affluent men
Knew grandeur; their mark found architectural fashion.

Now some remain with sage and pathetic towers,
And turrets. But not all in decay.
Stone, marble, and oak persist
Even against those who have lost through death
A drive to inhabit palaces.

Seventy-five years the lumberjacks cut pine,
Crossroads, sidings; and cities building,
And sawmills spewing shingles, lumber.

Raftsmen drove pieces through
Dangerous river narrows. Assembled
Acres-wide rafts in the St. Croix and Wisconsin;
Riding them down. Forty-foot steering oars—
Hell in white water. Take them sections apart, boys,
Come down in pieces. Ride it through!

Billions of board feet,
Barons in clover,
Knapp-Stout, Weyerhauser, Connors, and Goodman,
Sawyer and Paine, and what have you;
Living it up on Main Street,
High, wide and handsome.
And God help us.

Hardly any pioneers arrived
Unmotivated by what they interpreted
As God's will.

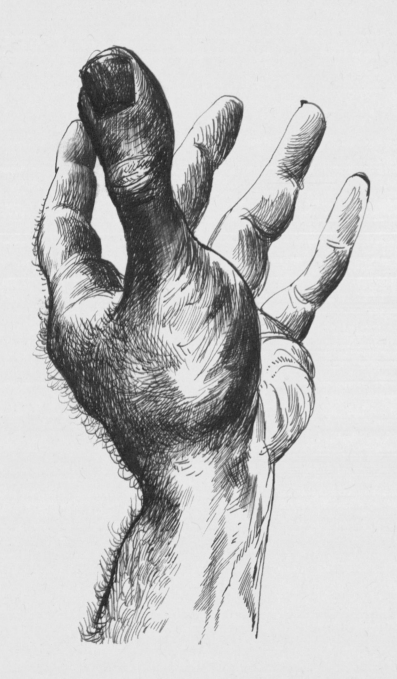

The Woodcutter - Bailey's Harbor
Aaron Bohrod

If I am lonely in Wisconsin
It is never the fault of the people
For my friends are in every town.

I have journeyed
Through thirty years of restless movement
To visit Wisconsin places.

I have gone often in the cause of art
To meet artists or writers
Or to share a community play.

The art with the most blood is in the people—
No elitist I, nor have I ever been—
It is the grassroots where the essence of art
Most joyously flourishes.

I attach art to the well-being of America,
For I have seen farmers happily writing poems,
And whole communities participating
In music and drama.

How can a nation be weak
With those dedicated to art
Counted by millions in country and city places?

If I am lonely in Wisconsin it is not because
No one has said come here
Be with us today.

Yet in loneliness I have watched as on a high crag
Waiting a vast upspringing of people
In behalf of art.

A lonely nightwatcher sensing loneliness;
Yet is my loneliness of love.

I have been with you for an hour or a day—
In joy with your joy
Accepting art in your country places.

In tears and laughter I have watched the people
Yet I have known what loneliness was
Because I desired the same joy
For all America.

John Curry from Kansas
Brought his art to Wisconsin
Inspiring country artists;

And Aaron Bohrod when Curry had gone

Went as I did to the towns

Speaking to the people about their art.

Of such concern was a great university the mother.

But if I am lonely it is more

Of the mood of the land.

It is loneliness of wild roadways

And the silence of those

Who were here long ago.

Of the people I am filled with joy and doubt

And wonder.Of the hills I am only a part

In their blue mystery.

I hear echoes through stone.

My loneliness is more the loneliness

Of wanting to know, to become,

To be a part of.

My spirit responds to rain and wind,

And to snow falling in silent woods;

Of birdsfoot violets on sandy hillsides,

And of orange puccoon and small buttercups.

My loneliness is not of people,

For the people are growing in art.

My loneliness is more of small weedgrown graveyards,

And forgotten aspiring men and women.

Where are those to whom the old graves

Belong?

I wandered lonely down a country road

I saw the purple grosbeak in the tree

I heard the cardinal calling from the wood

And knew that evening solitude

Was my own greatest good.

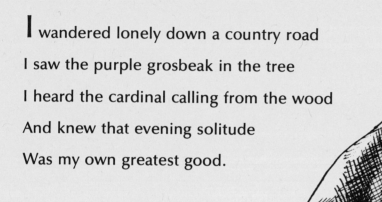

Walking through a newly plowed field, the birds

ahead flying up and then back and down as I

pass. Walking in rain that comes suddenly on a very hot

afternoon of dust, the pelt, the sensation of

great, leaping joy, the glory of wet clothing.

In such moments are we most conscious of water

and of earth. All thought of tilling, of working,

of dying, becomes as nothing when there is only

earth and water.

Town Square, Baraboo — Aaron Bohrod

Who aged earth and water,
Controlled time
Deified space?

Earth and water
Taken in their own being
Are recognizable
As sweat wiped from the face
Of a harvester.

Star,
Above the high, far river bluffs,
Lead to safe haven
All small wild creatures
On this night of Christian charity.

With cracking air
The frost vamps down
From hill to valley,
And lies silent upon white, ice-stiff grasses.
Small creatures of dark hill and tree
Need haven in men's hearts
Who could provide in easy-spoken
Peace on Earth
Space for small creatures crouching, clinging,
In deep winter travail.

Star,
Lead us men in memory
To those small beauties
Such humble creatures men supply:
Young rabbits romping in a meadow
In soft spring,
And winter birds
Watched into warmer sun,
And singing praises
For survival.

I saw how you regarded them
And they you, with slurred eyes—
Green eyes and lizard dark
Of jade and murked amber.

This wild flower road in back country—
It's a falltime scene, color in purple and god of gold,
Wild grasses cast in bronze, and brown, opened weed pods,
Wind in a dry rattle of summer death
Among unleafed boughs.

I, walking here, bring to this roadside setting
My own memory of splendid boyhood responses.
I am alone to observe the death of summer,
And later I will walk this road
To witness the advent of a starker season.

The roads here are meant for solitude.
They wind the hillsides swinging up;
And at a small crest cut the shoulder,
And stop and look backward into the deep valley
And thread of a dark river.

Along this road almost no human sign.
I seek nothing and man has small relationship to me
Only the way I respond is filled with question.
People have been my reason for life,
But on this country roadway in autumn
There is enough of meaning.

Only myself a sounding harp for wind,
And devourer of roadside flowers and autumn dyes.
I see a mailbox beside the road, I pause.
Mailboxes are as country weathervanes
Testing the directions of people. I have seen them
Mounted in rural-fanciful ways on plows;
On an upthrust snake of logchain; welded on an old pump
That I suppose once watered thirsty cattle.
I have noted mailboxes on posts from Sears,
On knotty, crude, lengths of unbarked pine.
Mailboxes are of people and mailboxes
Are tokens of human hopes and fears;
These I know well. But here I pause:
This box is an old one and the name faded some.
I cannot read it—Morgan or Miller,
Impossible to tell. But a bird has been here
This morning and the door is open.
There is already a sprinkling of grass and down.
Tomorrow the mailman may disturb
A nest-building bluebird; let me trust
That no mail merely addressed to occupant
Is deposited in this lonely, small, sanctuary.

Aaron Bohrod

If I were a Whitman, I might tell of my wanderings.

Here among old houses and night-lonely streets, among the

remnants of wild dreams and ancient logs in streams,

I might tell in great poetry how I arrived seeking,

and of what I discovered in valley and on hill.

If I could relate the heart of a past generation

where old men and women walk in memory and tell

in hesitating words of young hopes.

Michigan

Coming and coming slurrs the rocks,
Fills potholes and out.

On South Point we waited;
It was from here we could see the island,
The rock, and swarming gulls.

It is Apriltime of storms.
The lake-winter wind
Exposes its steel teeth.
The trap springs back on itself.

The water to my feet,
I feel Michigan's early spring knife.
It is thrust and cut but I do not move,
My belief is in water and in wind.

My mother said, the Lord
Would certainly preserve both man and beast,
But it was her
I had chief faith in,
For she walked with me on Sunday mornings
In the springtime woods,
And explained earth's mysterious spell
Of dogtooth violet spear
Through moist soil and leafy mould,
And how columbines became reality
On cliffs.

She said that God
Most loved farmers
And sanctified the earth
Even in drought and flood,
For God sent scorching sun and pelting rains.
Surely my mother was
Of close relationship with God,
For she loved all things growing of earth,
But she accepted also withering death.

It was difficult for me
To find soul solace within walls
When a cornfield temple
Seemed a better habitation
For the Great Spirit.

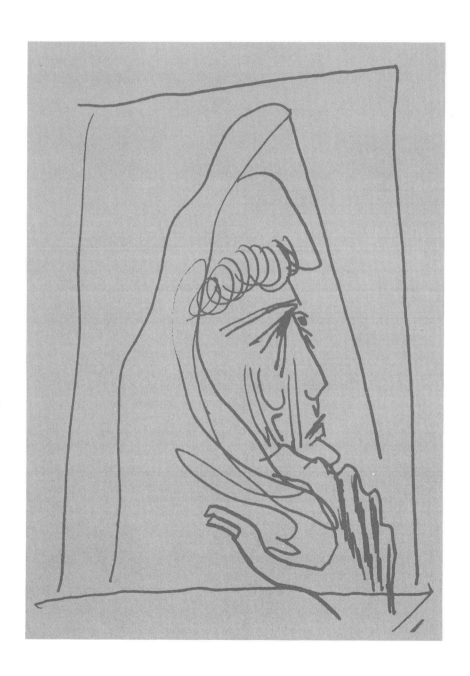

In youth I lived and felt the earth,
My bare feet thrust into the stirrups
Of a two-row corn cultivator
Animal-pulled.
We had no tractor
Boy and beasts knew spewing earth
And smell of green corn.

Oh blacksuited man of God,
I am not sacrilegious
Because I hold that out-of-doors
Is man's most fitting place of worship.
For I have never feared
The speared lightnings and tearing winds.
My mother created of me a primitive
And adjusted my thought
To spears of new growth
Or to far stars and manifestations of spring.

Yet could she believe there was a God
To cause winds in the night,
And to multiply my boyhood wonder:
Of all earth and sky,
Of all woodland vine and flower,
Of all bark and wood and forest track,
Of instincts which I now possess,
And owe to the past in which I knew
That there did exist a pasture God.

My plow was broken against stone
I had no other
To scarify the southern meadow.
I left it for weeds
That in fall
Became golden and glorious.

The stone remained,
My plow is not repaired.
As tiller I am a failure,
Yet the earth may benefit
From a fallow season,
And I will respond
Even as a harp in wind
To autumn.

The large black stove was my friend

On sharp winter dawns.

I dressed before it often before school,

Backing closer and closer,

I scorched my pants one morning;

Perforce I wore the brown stain on through the spring.

In summer the old stove was removed to the shed;

The room thereafter appeared to lack a soul.

I pondered often the enigma

Of objects that disappear suddenly from a young life,

And what emptiness then takes place

When morning rituals of warmth become memory fragments,

And central furnaces will not suffice

To embellish a youth's comprehension

Of friendly relationship with a country room

Dominated by a black motherly monster

Heated red.

I came, in fact, from a line of oak-burning folk.

No other winter wood would do.

My grandfather said nothing would warm his bones

Save woodscut oak.

I only wish I could go now to those same woods

To cut oak firewood and later see it blaze

In a roundoak wood heater where the men,

After the chores were done, gathered

To spin the day's work into fiction.

He died
And I humbly
Strove to assume his shadow.
He was a large, kind, and puzzling man
Who swung through his lifeway
On crutches.
Yet he made
The usual chords of society
Retreat to silence
Against his loud cries
Demanding man's participation
In a ritual of art.

I saw him often
And desired deep talk
But he led me usually to a night hilltop
Where wordless,
We stared together
Into a quiet sky.

I, his disciple,

He my master.

I gladly called him so

For he taught me that people

Were my necessity.

He taught me to know

The starved loneliness in man

And to ease it a little

With art and poetry.

Now he is gone

And I left with constant striving;

Yet my shadow is minute

Against the backdrop

Of a hillside night

Where a dream of man's magnificence

Lay unspoken

Beyond wordless viewing

Of white far stars.

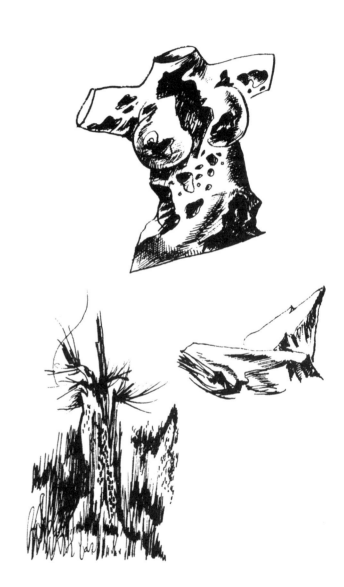

Indian Cemetery
MADELAINE ISLAND
Aaron Bohrod

Spiderwort thrives in blue
Along old railroad tracks.

Tell me friend:
Why do blue flowers flourish
Beside railroad right-of-ways?

I have always wondered
Because blue flowers evoke
A long-ago face staring in puzzlement
From a dusty train window
At the strew of blue blossoms,
Swiftly passed and never understood.

I know the draw
Of deep Wisconsin earth,
And I have chronicled its story.
I know the magnet of soil,
Of valley and hillslope.
The proof lies in forgotten graveyards
Among Wisconsin hills.

I know how the wind
Can stir the appendages of earth things,
And how the roots of trees
Understand the needs of earth.

I know also how the night wind sounds
In cedars above old graves.

During Depression years families were moved off their land by the government.

The land was submarginal and the people were often starving.

But homesteads had been long inhabited and wrench of departure was pathetic.

Back in the hills were old graves where the first settlers were buried.

Aaron Bohrod

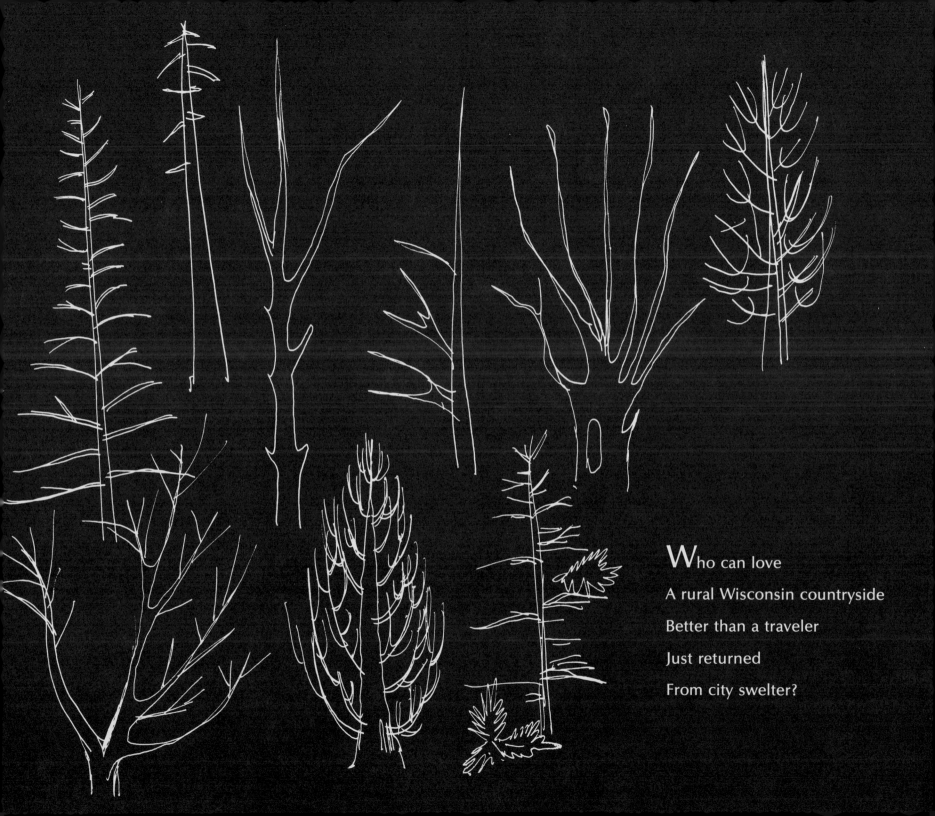

Who can love
A rural Wisconsin countryside
Better than a traveler
Just returned
From city swelter?

What items on early winter mornings

Do I consider—

It is a silent city

That has forgotten Christmas.

The midnight gird of lights has gone,

Death has come to the pavement,

And I think only of one Christmas morning:

When I, a little boy, cherished a thorntree

Cut from a Kansas copse

In place of evergreen—

Branch-wrapped with green paper crepe,

Cherished by me

Because I had made it,

And because it made a beloved person

Smile.

Later in my own place

I see there are no birds yet

Under the blue spruce.

But they will arrive,

For I have seen how they endure the winter.

For them I have scattered humble offerings of seeds,

And they have become more trusting

As winter becomes more permanent.

It is I who have had so much of winter joy,

Searching the city

For signs of my understanding;

Wherein men and animals,

And mix of earth and water,

Will overcome death hovering over pavements

And hooded among walls;

And will survive, preserving reverance,

For mornings traveled and looked back to

Through things done and tenderly

Remembered.

What celebrations

Have I made

To pre-dawn meadow-mists,

To final stars,

To far and isolated birdsongs,

To the sound of the rivers,

To the soft brush of grasses,

To sounds of barnyard labors.

I leave night at the woodedge

And explore

An emerging Wisconsin morning.

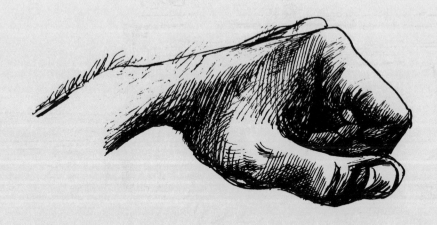

Creation is of God,

And through Him,

Of an old man's hands.

All activities are a celebration of man or God.

It is nature that man celebrates best.

Nature was provided as a trust to man.

His celebrations are in honor of its primitiveness, and of his own feelings toward land and

water, plants and birds.

He approaches the small lake with reverence; he watches the flight in the sky, the insects

from the valley places.

He regards small flowers with awe, and in his celebrations he signals the seasons.

Man in Wisconsin is nature's child.

Oh man!

Draw in the tokens of your reverence: the country roads and weeds in ditches, the circles

in backwaters, wood-tread trails that animals have made; draw out the stone but remember

the blue glacier; know that you are the protector who must revere.

Watch waterways and hold your court with conscience.

A circus street parade still forms for me

Each time I pass the riverside sheds

Of Ringling's old winter quarters in Baraboo.

They stand as though awaiting the return

Of the great menagerie from the summer tours;

As though when the circus train draws onto the siding

Everything in the sleepy town

Transforms instantly to showmanship magic.

There is Baraboo, home mother of circuses,

And Delevan, mother of circuses,

And Lake Geneva, mother of circuses,

And small Evansville, mother of circuses.

Why did Wisconsin nurse so well

This leveler and delighter of society,

This common man's passion,

This rich man's pride and companion?

All gladly shared hard bleacher seats.

Why did the circus train wheels pause,

Great acts and performing families lose identity,

And legendary circus elephants—

Coco, Baldy, Little Charlie, Romeo and Queen—

Become almost forgotten legends?

To a country boy in my time

The great Ringling circus was fire

To a winter of waiting.

Well we have tatters and the remains.

Old circus rail cars wait on a spur at Baraboo.

Wheels and wagons with carvings by the great wood-masters

Are waiting at the circus museum.

And there is a menagerie

That once a year moves out to Milwaukee,

But the age has closed.

Never again will the mighty brothers

Who began with a Classic and Comic Concert Company—

And grew to a Big Top that covered all America—

Never again, will the great five

Roam Baraboo streets after a summer on the road.

Al Ringling's house is the Elk's Club.

The Ringling Theater now shows movies.

All of the old circus crowd is dead,

And the Big Top will never rise again.

Small towns often possess great mansions
Built by stubborn developers
Who hoped to win a race against death,
And leave their memorials on forgotten street corners
In places that never quite made the grade.

PARLOR
Hat Shoppe

yellow

white

Aaron Bohrod

Bristol.

Barns are for boys on rainy days,
And for men on Sunday afternoons.

Barns are for insects, and farm women
With egg baskets.

An old barn board
Is a memory-sliver of wind and time.

Aaron Bohrod.
Daleyville

A hillside graveyard

Of wrecked old cars

Makes obscene

The forgotten spangle of a field

Where once meadow flowers

Gave an old woman,

Gazing from her farmhouse window,

Her only springtime joy.

Small evening noises

Are of restless swallows and

Swooping insects

Around decaying barns.

Of brick, stained wood and steel

No nature temple,

It breaks the gentle contour

Of a wooded hill.

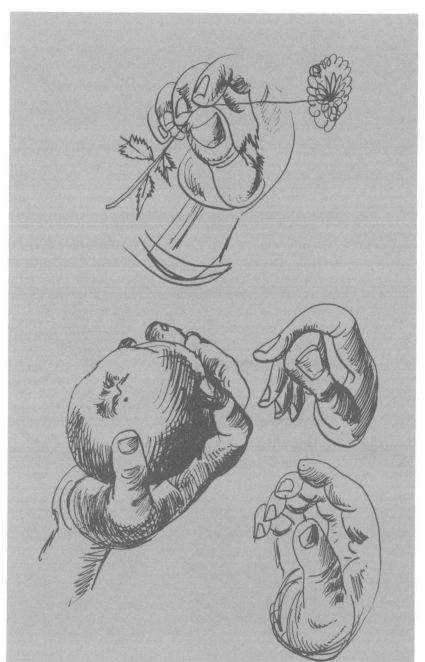

A friendly hand in the warm night
Touching me;
Lips therein saying:
How is it, star-reader?
How is it, reader of night skies,
Star-reader?

I saw the white stars
Above and below the night.
I read them of their coming and going,
And I heard the bird in the ineluctable wood.

I saw the man as he came first to the land,
Heaving and breaking.
I saw his hands
Curved to the black plow wood.
I heard the man speak.

He spoke strange words,
There was also the bird.

Cry, cry, bird,
Read, star-reader,
Come, man, to tear the earth.
Vision your heart against bitter roots.
Vision your hands at ninety,
Curved emptily against the remembered plow.

Curved to the flow of toil.
Work, labor man,
Rip the earth,
Let the trees burn in continuous smoulder;
Smart the eyes and cursing,
Belabor the stolid ox.

Star-reader.
I witnessed yesterday the dregs of your toil—
Yoke on a dusty barn wall,
And broken, iron, oxen shoes.

I saw the white stars, and wings
Disturbed my reading.
I hear the lips saying:
How is it, star-reader?
How is the night from above? How do the stars lie so silent?
Why is the mirror-lake so still?
Comes never the wind? Ever?

Show the man and the woman,
Who in the summer,
Were here at this place,
He with hand on her white breast.
Read on
With the bird in the wood
Crying.

I awoke on clear morning and said

I will certainly do something great today,

I will move a mountain

Or at least cause a bell to chime

Celebrating some minor victory.

Instead, near Spring Green,

I crossed a star-flowered prairie,

Sat down in the middle of tall grass,

And simply stared upward

At white clouds in a spring sky.

A Wisconsin meadow

In spring,

With shooting stars

And sweet star grasses,

Can make a fulfilled astronomer

Of any earthbound, astral,

Day seeker.

Waters within waters,
Earth within earth,
One drop a cosmos.

Adjust microscope knobs,
Look within and observe wonders.

One flake of earth—
Note its biological reality,
Then magnify it
To become a universe.

Water a drop,
Earth a flake,
Man filled with knowing
Of both small and great.
Place yourself against earth and water.
Reap the wind on the hill,
Find meadow at the crest,
Unviolated for a thousand years.

You become aware of earth and water,
A droplet,
A flake, tells it all.

But you know little
Of rivers and mountains
Of being all
Of becoming nothing.

The still small lake,
Where lonely loons
Haunt the eastern shore.

Small lake,
Lake of loons,
Lake of wood violets,
Lake of water reeds,
Lake of lotus,
Lake of fern and willow,
Lake of night stillness,
Lake of birds,
Lake of reflected star,
Lake of canoe sadness.

Lake of morning,
Lake of evening,
Lake of names for sounds,
For women,
For fish,
For Red Men,
For early settlers,
Landlookers.

Created of Sibelius music
And night mist.
We drift waiting.

The lake has no name,
It is unviolated, pure.
It has no name.
It is primitive pureness
In the heart of wood.

I remember best a single bird call, no matter what kind . . . possibly a cardinal, coming from the edge of a wood below the house. Silence except for the clear whistle. A sense of depth, sureness. Faint light across the meadow. There is wind. The mind is free, and the touch of everything becomes painful through awareness. These are Wisconsin moments to be experienced only before the real day begins, and when one is very, very much alone. These are moments—infinity—between man and the grasses, and the departing stars. Love of place is created before dawn, of silence and accents of far sound, so poignant they become living memories. Perhaps country people know early morning best. But city folk may feel the keen touches of nature even more deeply.

If there is a river, its voice is eternal.
There is no stopping or turning. Man is
alone with the river, and with whatever
the single, far, birdsong stimulates in
him.

A grain field only now spring-plowed,

Is festival for small birds.

They crowd clean furrows

And fly up as I walk near them,

Clouding an April sky.

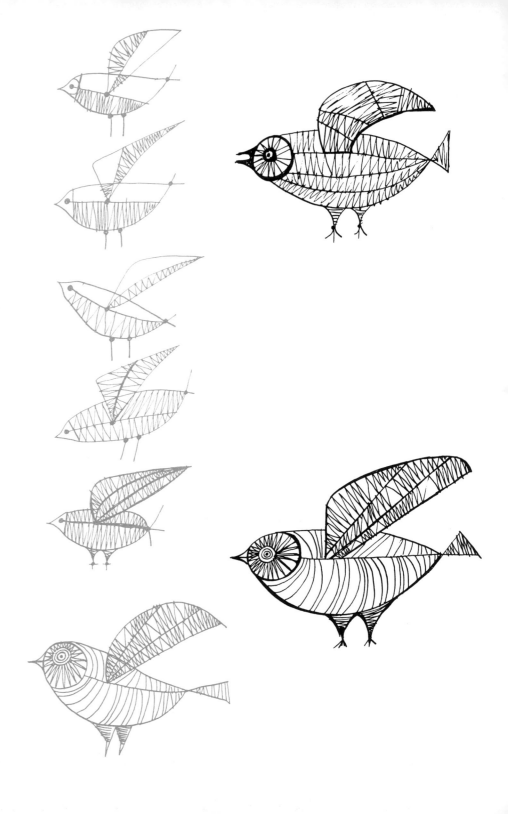

The birds of winter

Possess hungers beyond pain.

They cling to the brick parapet

Uttering small, sorrowing sounds

As I walk past them to my office.

Spiked wind has little pity

For small winter-desperate birds.

No inclination towards comfort

For these wild ones who

Cling against brick walls,

Dying in ashcans.

Oh mourning dove
I heard you in the night,
Lonely echo of my heart.

When I observe Wisconsin winter

Stark against bleak branches and snow

And notice how my neighbor

Makes careful way across his icy pasture,

I think that sure death has arrived

And plant-time victims buried deep beneath crust,

Will never again know quickened roots

Searching a taste of long-forsaken spring.

My own steps, crusty and hesitant,

Follow his as we go to the far woodlot.

Today we must cut oak, our joint pile is sparse,

New oak splits easily in zero cold.

He swings his axe with precise finesse,

The hard bite splits down the tight grain,

And snap of frozen sap and broken fibres

Heartens me as I remember that hard oak wood

Cut in cold winter, blazes well.

I die of winter,

Yet the snow at the gate is

Pure

Beyond believing.

Black Earth
Aaron Bohrod

Skeleton reeds
Rattle in January dance
As the arrow of the wind
Cuts the heart
Of the marsh.

Soldier spears of marsh grass
Stalagmited by last night's freezing rain,
Thrust up a million shining blades
Against my destroying boots.

The grass army shatters in early sun,
And the track of my going
Leaves fragmented glass-grass armor
In a narrow spear-lined path.

Broken reeds
And dark weeds.
Meadows of snow
Reflecting violet shadows.

Balsam branches
Bent to earth
By last night's thick pluck
Of heaven-fell geese.

Who plucks the skies
To bring white drifts
Into my woods?

Who sends seeds for birds
In dark winter?

Winter marsh.
We walk on frozen marsh seep,
Rattle dry milkweeds
And star-weed grayed brittle.
I gather bunches of marsh grass,
Dried cattails, red dogwood.
I linger beside a dead stump,
Fragile with dry rot and break it open.

Lichens grow on an old willow;
I collect them and now
I place these marsh mementos
On an old old board
Torn from an aged marsh barn.
These dried winter pods and stems
And the old board
Will decorate my study wall,
And in fall
When the Canada geese return,
I will remember how the wind can pain
And the marsh rattle on a January day.

Small-town Wisconsin

Seen at night through slow falling snow,

As though the heart of the village

Has ceased pulsing for a moment,

So that the gentle white form,

Street and firm shrouded houses,

May be seen as in

A quiet death vision.

Streets of small-town Wisconsin

Turn very silent at dusk.

Once, long ago, the man with the long stick

Walked the street, carefully,

As though not to disturb shadows,

Touching strange, small, streetlamps

Giving birth

To unreal illumination.

Wisconsin Dells
Aaron Bohrod

Small-town Wisconsin

Echoes often the past steps

Of ones who dreamed a vaster grandeur.

Jail Alley. MINERAL POINT

Aaron Bohrod

Aaron Bohrod
MINERAL POINT

MADISON, WIS

Mineral Point — Aaron Bohrod

This crossroads,

Unpainted houses and

Sleeping dogs,

Was once the center of a certain world.

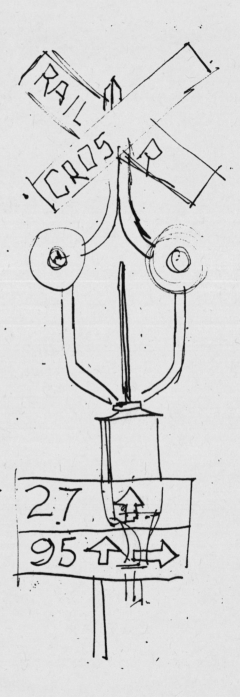

Mineral Point
Aaron Bohrod

On a May morning, my friend pointed out to me the many variations of dooryard tree

plantings, and said then that he could always tell something about the folks who lived in

a certain farmhouse, by the way the trees grew: near the house, in a line behind the barn,

over around the edge of a field. Trees, he said, were as people's souls. He suggested

that certain kinds of trees denoted the places from which settlers had come. Trees they

were fond of in the old home places were the kind they wanted in their new surroundings.

Also, he reminded me that there were many salesmen in the early days who circulated

through the countryside selling saplings: fruit trees or shade trees. For dooryard trees

were very highly regarded. Sometimes a tree was planted when a child died, or a mother.

When I pass old farmhouses I think I always look first at the trees.

Aaron Bohrod

There is an uncompromising reality
In dooryard trees.
Once I saw an old cedar,
Planted a hundred years ago,
To bear witness that a child
Had once lived and died in a small farmhouse.

Aaron Bohrod

Long breaks of willow
Planted beside fields,
Might indicate a better potato crop
If sandy soil
Drifts in wind.

And cedars grouped near farmhouses
Deflect northwestern storms.

Yet given their practical applications
Trees planted by country folk
To break sharp winds
Have for me an arrow-stroke
Of sadness.
Those who set them out
Are surely now dead,
And, I wonder,
If their existence is fittingly recalled
By cedars at a dooryard,
Or willows at the edges
Of a sand-country potato farm.
The old attach themselves
Somehow to trees.

They relate

How grandfather pocketed a sack of apple seeds,

Out from York State in the '50s;

Planted an orchard the very first day

His wagon rolled onto Empire Prairie.

Went into an oak opening and dug seedlings

For dooryard shade and some protection.

Old people always speak of trees:

The black locust broke

In the great ice storm of '23.

They speak of trees

As of children or loved parents,

And use trees somehow

To mark moments in time.

In aging clarity of memory,

Old folks cling to trees

To interpret their lives.

I searched for stories in the rain

And found them under tamarack tree:

Scratchings, burrowings and tracks

Of wild things that had written

Tales of their struggles.

Tamaracks rust in fall,

And on early mornings with frost,

The wide marshland has rusted with them,

Overnight.

Tree branches crack

On an evening of frozen rain,

As I wander

At the edge of winter wood.

Trinity Church
Waupun AB.

Wisconsin centennial church,
Those who do not revere tradition
Plan to murder you next year.

They'll have you down.
Your old walnut pews
Are destined to become seats
In a country bowling alley.
Your stained glass,
Is already coveted by a tavern.

Some fought for you,
But not enough loved your sagging shape.
In your place there will be a steel story
And prefabricated laminated beams.
Those who hollowed your front steps
May not be well remembered
By a new village god;
Nor those wedded and buried
From your sanctuary.

They'll have you down.
And in far less than a hundred years,
The new temple will find
Its own kind of dust.

The old church stands on central village stage

Against the magic nightcloth of the street.

It was here we once produced

Great Marlowe's Doctor Faustus—

Mephistopheles stalked center aisle,

And Faustus was strongly portrayed by the rector.

We revealed the classic image of Helen of Troy,

She in a hard, tight, spot

High on a ladder in the sanctuary.

For a little while fine theatre came to the village church.

God's temple became also a temple for art:

An old village church

Became all things for all men,

And portrayed both the strength of art

And the continuity of generations.

This small, white, lonely church
Stands at a crossroad
With a long forgotten name.
Yet masters of the shipbuilding craft
Built this small, now decaying wonder.
They came from coastal Maine
To settle in Wisconsin woods—
They were clipper ship builders—
And the timbers they hewed
For rafters
Are joined in perfect ship joints.

Rural folks don't gather
At this brave old church nowadays,
They have a new one down the road.
But they will not destroy it either,
An old man full of wrath,
Guards it. But someday newness will be above God,
Wolves of progress will win
And ship-joined church rafters
Are doomed to lie behind somebody's barn
Until weeds overgrow and hide
Their perfectly crafted beauty.

Women are Wisconsin heroes;

Their faith and dedication have no boundaries.

Without their concern, Wisconsin would be a desert

Where art blooms only as a dwarfed desert cactus.

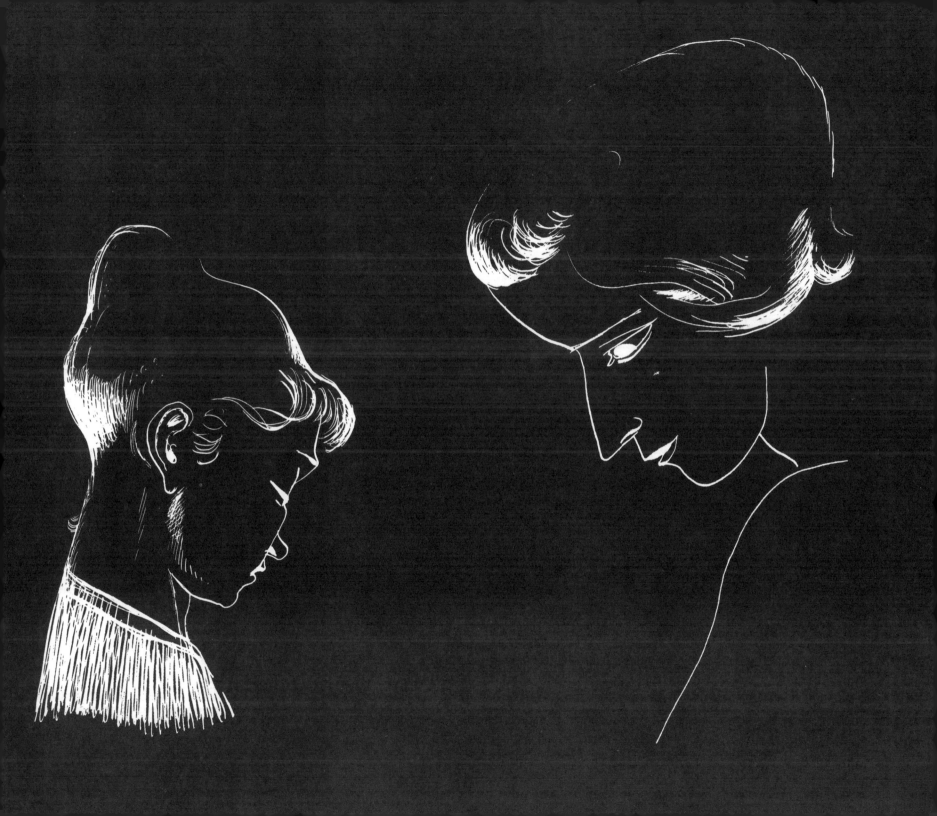

Women are culture bearers.

It is they who have rescued art

In time of wars and manic materialistic peace.

Again and again I have seen it happen:

A courageous woman leading her town

To perform some impossible task;

The renovation or salvation

Of some threatened aspect of community,

Beauty or tradition,

Or establishment of programs

Wherein children might see something

Of the wonder of art.

A bridal bouquet of white thornblossoms

Plucked from haws on a Wisconsin hill,

Was the wish of this woman

Who desired to be wed

On the very, very high land

Above the Wisconsin River.

She was indeed wed by a caring man,

She in patched blue jeans and gingham shirt,

Holding white hillside flowers:

The whole tableau

Against a blue June morning sky.

I can't say I ever saw a more radiant bride,

And her young man whose hair was long

Tenderly aided his aging mother

Over stone and goat meadow,

While in junipers round about

Waxwings uttered a wedding

Serenade.

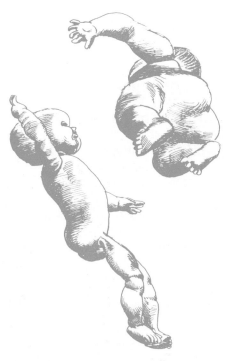

Wisconsin woman,

Writers now set forth

To grant belated glory

To your pioneer strength,

And make your passionate heroic idealism

Reason enough for reform.

You have shaken off

A mastery of overlords;

But in your recognized role

Do not forget that you also

Owe earth her beauty

And that many will still share with you:

A caring among pasture flowers

A clear breath of city air

An evening amidst trembling corn

A colored sunup above misty hills.

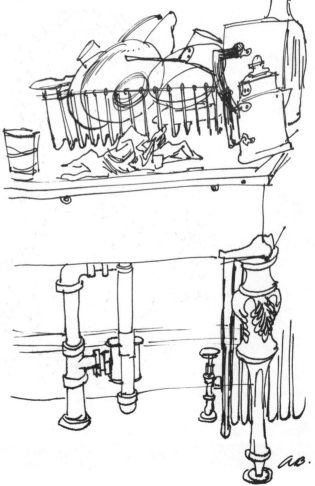

Give Wisconsin earth
The new vitality of your liberation,
And lead us again to an ancient regard
For primitive purity.

For it was you, Wisconsin woman,
Who set the trails
And cured the sick,
Made bearable habitations in log shacks.

Now in the power of your new strength
Let Wisconsin woman
Discover her own heroic place.

Mayflowers

Along a woods road home from church,

And children

Carrying the stems and leaves as a

Pretend umbrella, for

Make-believe rain.

Long ago an astronomer friend

Took me at night to the Yerkes Observatory.

I supposed that I might stare through

The world-famous telescope,

and perceive rapid answers

To my bothering questions about the universe.

Instead, I heard only soft camera clicks

As the monster casually photographed

The constellations.

I very often try to imagine

How the wilderness that was Wisconsin

Might now appear to the young Muir

Were he to come and stand at evening

Above Mendota

And remember that he was once in love

With scum-free water

And old elms.

I wish I had known these great men:

Muir walking, burdened with his wooden inventions,

To the state university;

And Wright dreaming strange structures

In the Wyoming Valley.

I wish I might have been beside Muir

When, departing, he gazed backward at the university,

And knew what truth it had granted

To his youth and dreams.

And I would have cherished standing beside Wright

When he, too, looked backward at his alma mater

And knew that he must seek his own truth

In farther, city locations.

Broken anvil

And an unseen force beating it

With a furious hammer

Keeping hammer-time to dreams.

Back in the hills

The anvil sound and muffled voices

Are one with old and decayed buildings.

They preserve the anvil sound

of forgotten smiths,

And the doorways where the horses

Entered to be shod

Seem sunken and much too low.

Forgotten smiths once beat out useful items

Hanging often now as curios or luck signs.

I do not understand how earth

Can permit anvil sound to ring out

Against nothing.

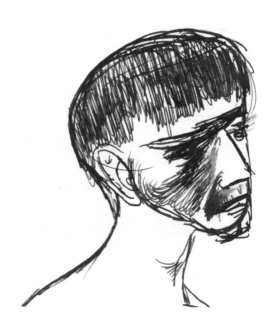

Against the dark hill:

Taliesin.

Deserted.

They have fled.

Oh bold one,

Lonely one,

Lost one,

Deserted one,

Now.

Along a country way

Wound the slow, wagon-led cortege

Of one who loved roadside flowers,

And transported green evergreen branches

And woodland blossoms

To create the reality:

A continuity of man,

And of hillside time.

This was the funeral procession of Wright, the architect. The simple cortege moved over a country road, the wagon, horse-drawn, to the small family rural chapel. The grave marker is but a thrust of country stone, unshaped.

There is a cry

Of nighthawks

Over Taliesin

Nighthawks unseen

Crying and booming

And under a fieldstone

In a country chapel burying ground

Rests the master

Of space, time and materials.

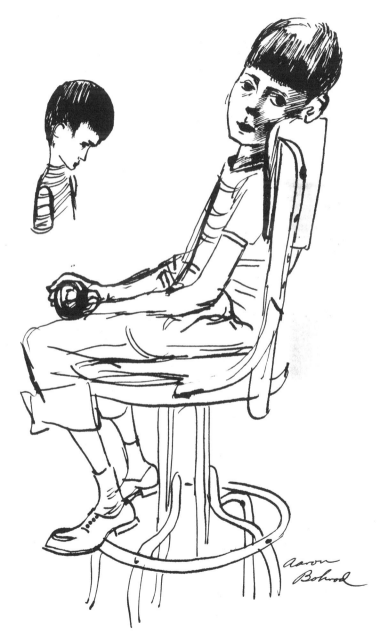

Sauk City
Aaron Bohrod

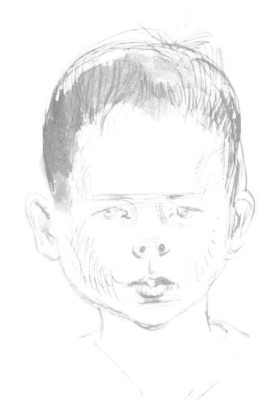

EAGLE

Aaron Bohrod
BAYFIELD

This precious intervene

Between brook and woodland

Is a slender meadow,

Knife-shaped,

Spotted with sand-country lupine.

Bent bows of huntsmen
Haunt now ancient trails
Where deer and elk
Once footed through a forest fortress
To drink the clear river.

Springtime plowing one year
Uncovered stone arrowpoints
In the south field—
Many make a modern hobby
Collecting century-chipped artifacts.

Over nearer the Crawfish River,
Some boys digging in clay,
Uncovered fragmented cooking pots
That had strange-curious carvings.

The ancient peoples
Were here through copper and stone,
Stone-rough and with rude scoops of wood
Created the effegies in sacred burial spots.

A benchmark hidden in deep woods,

A trail tree with Indian-tied branches,

To point out an obliterated track.

No man, red or white, can now find its path.

Time has eroded all.

No more the sound of moccasins.

I once sat quietly

With the wise man of the Oneidas,

And he told me

How the Orchard Indians,

The Oneidas,

Arrived in Wisconsin

From New York State

After selling their lands

For a penny an acre.

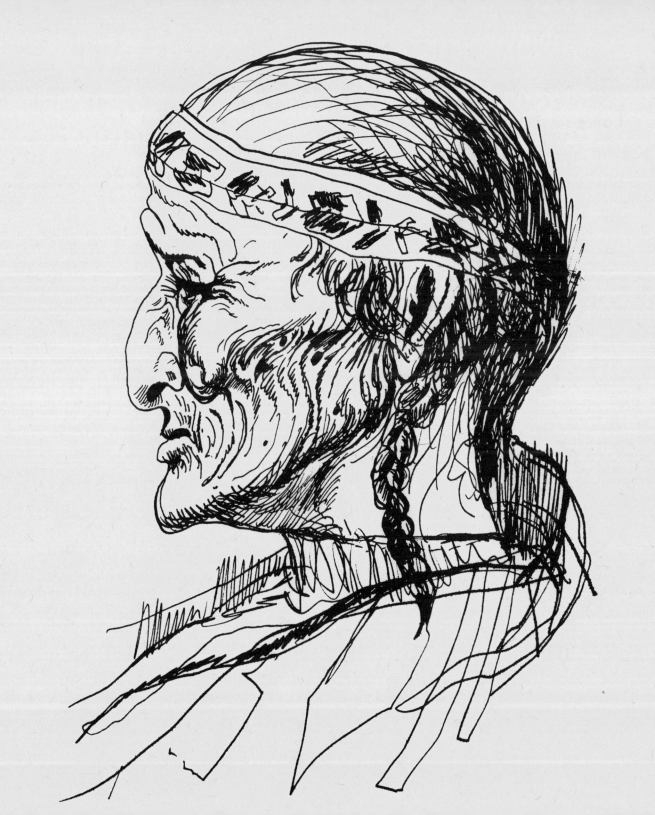

These hills were once bare of juniper

But wild birds have planted berry seed,

Juniper spreads its creeping green

Across the highest goat prairies.

The ancient peoples
Who were our brothers;
Who celebrated spring at Aztalan,
And Man-Mound Park,
And Castle Rock,
And Neenah,
And Lizard Mound Park,
And on the firmer shores
Of the Horicon Marsh,
Reliefed the Wisconsin land
With symbols.

I knew an amateur anthropologist
Who argued the mound builders
Were Druid-like,
And worshipped sun and moon.
He visited the effigy mounds
Searching for evidence:
How the ancient Indians lined the mounds
With the heavenly bodies.

He thought he saw
How the mounds pointed the stars
And the sunrise
On Midsummer's morning.

On Eagle Hill
Above the university,
On primitive hallowed earth,
I stand on the great rock,
Mendota unseen far below,
But the spirit of the waters is
Felt in the wind.

On Eagle Hill
I sense the ceremonial rising
Of man-ghosts, those
Who created the conical mound.

In the wind
Which brings faint sound,
I hear voices chanting
The song of earlier peoples
Whose buried dead make this mound
Above Mendota.
They knew the same silence,
Perhaps more profoundly,
That tonight sweeps me
With unearthly lyrical sadness.

These broken departing red peoples

Who left the Wisconsin land beaten

Bound for more western country

Alien to hearts.

They have memory-scarred the rivers

Lakes and woods

With traces of a people's being.

Faint accounts of old trails

Leading to marsh and plain,

Have endowed the oldest ones, and they alone,

Using uncertain knowledge from hearsay and legend,

They can tell where moccasined feet

Wore deeper pathways

In the unbroken earth.

I have tried at times

To follow their tracks,

Have fancied that I saw evidence

On stone or beside waterways on ancient stumps,

That here perhaps a dim trace

Led to a rich hunting country,

Or into wide marshes and stands

Of rich red cranberries and bending wild rice.

Winnebago woman,
Winnebago people in Chicago starve.
Little enough food,
Deprivation of soul.
Four thousand Winnebago people,
Remnants of a proud tribe,
Lords once of two million acres,
Gone to the Big Town,
To Sandberg's Hog Butcher City;
They left woodland and deer trail,
To go to Sandberg's City of the Big Shoulders,
The City of Easy Starvation,
And dead red pride.

Who knows the Winnebago in Chicago?
You come to alien land
In the City of Wind.
You are a people of the woods,
Marshes and wild cranberry.

Why do you drift now at the Dells,
Up from Chicago for summer dollars,
Waiting for death among bedraggled tatters,
Sorry shatters of Winnebago pride,
Lodges and cooking pots for curious eyes.

Somebody mutters:
Squaws are always fat.

Your men dance for the tourists,

Why do they not take you to your landright

Among woods and wild marsh cranberries?

When the summer ends

You will return to Sandberg's City,

Oh Winnebago woman

Daughter of the forest wind!

White brothers
Have you no pity for the earth
Where my forefathers followed narrow trails
Through still forests?

Have you no pity
For the waters of earth,
For singing birds,
For willow and sky,
Night silence?

Have pity on our land,
White brothers.
It was because of you
That prairie sod was ripped to rain,
Forests became gray stumps,
And from the hills back of barns
Waters went to taint pure lakes.

It was because of you

That murderous blue algae floated,

Strangling fish.

What can you do

To make your peace with earth?

Death cannot repair desolation,

Nor can multitudes of apartments

Take the place of eternal wilderness.

Where will man now find silence?

Take pity, white brothers

On earth and sky.

You are the strong ones:

Earth masters,

Have pity.

Have pity

On springtime and small flowers.

Old man
With shadowed blue eyes,
This wheel chair
Is not for you.

The open field is yours
With stubble
Turning under your bright share.

Or you with fine cattle
In a tight barn,
For you belong to earth
And your wheel chariot
Can never be your Case tractor,
Or legs for your morning ramble,
Seeking cows by the Kickapoo.

Yet we never speak of your enchainment,
Unspoken we accept your only locomotion
And a warmly remembered, earth-loving past.

Steam above Mendota,
As a feral zero wind
Slowly strangles the dark water
Into troubled insensibility.

Soon the ice fishermen,
The impervious ones,
Will arrive pulling small sleds.

They will come laughing and spinning wild tales.

On an afternoon in January
You will see them from high land
Assembled in faint colored knots
Far out on Mendota ice.

I have mingled with ice fishermen
Squatting above small, pulsing mouths,
Feeling with gloved fingers
The searching far below.

The wind is twisting and saw-toothed.
The cruel broomsweep of wind
Is heartless across the whole lake.
There is no hiding place on Mendota ice.

But the bottle is warm,
And hot coffee passes back and forth.

Here these sturdy personalities who wait
Above iced potholes,
Are of classic heroic cut.

Ice fishermen chiefly live for winter days.
The rapidly passed word is glorious:
She's frozen in good,
This Saturday we'll go for sure.

Ice fishermen are as no other men.

They find religion in slab-sided cold,
In primitive ice and knowledge
Of black waters beneath.
There is a pull of primitive man
In these jolly fellows who share and love
A deep and ritual life impulse.

I think of days among ice fishermen

With joy, as from my window I see

Steam rising above Mendota

And watch, day by day,

The darkened lake become motionless.

Ice Fishing, Lake Mendota

Iron on iron

Rock on rock

Rip of sod

Hymn to God

Axe on pine

This church

This earth

This Wisconsin world

Is mine.

1848 men cried freedom

And roots from embryos

In Norway and the Netherlands—

People crying:

Here it is

These hills

This valley

This link of woods

Is ours.

Iron on iron

Rock on rock

They came

They came.

Their names

Are monuments

Of wanting

Of having

Of having been

Of dying.

Iron on iron

Rock on rock

Iron on iron

Rock on rock.

God among pioneers

Was some small comfort against tears

When drought

Withered up a field

Of new corn.

God among pioneers

Drew faith from earth

And every tear

A vow to God:

Next year.

Aaron Bohrod

Old roads that pioneers once trod
Are often superhighways now
And figure-eights rape daiseyed pastures
Where meadow larks once flew toward the sky
And sang out morning.

The need of Wisconsin earth
Is man's hands
To crumble and make smooth.

The need of earth
Is a woman dropped to her knees
To sense reality of grass.

The need of earth
Is a landing of birds
And the freeing of water.

The need of earth

Is a man's hope of crops

And of his proud steps among new growth.

The need of earth

Is wildness left

In uncut fence corners.

The need of earth

Is the shape of man's mind

Searching the meaning of earth.

Under the peeled-apple moon

The lovers lay on light-dappled earth

While above them the corn crossed

Sabre leaves

And a night zephyr, give gentle action

To the duel.

The settler walked out to Wisconsin

From Connecticut,

And thrust,

Near Mount Horeb,

His walking stick of black locust

Into fertile earth.

He had come home, he said,

And was done with walking.

So, also, did Joseph of Aramathea.

Plant out the Holy Thorn in Britain,

And like Joseph's cudgel,

The black locust staff of Mount Horeb took root

And became a landmark

On the plain.

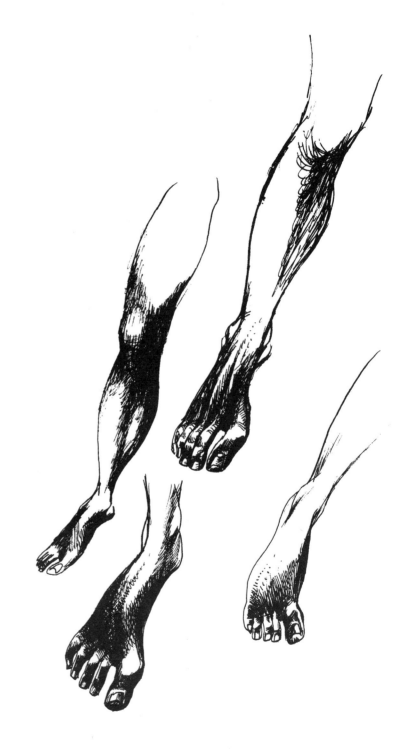

I went forth seeking tales; to me the old

Are the fearless oracles of literature.

The old ones have made the stories;

A man's hands tell how he misses his work.

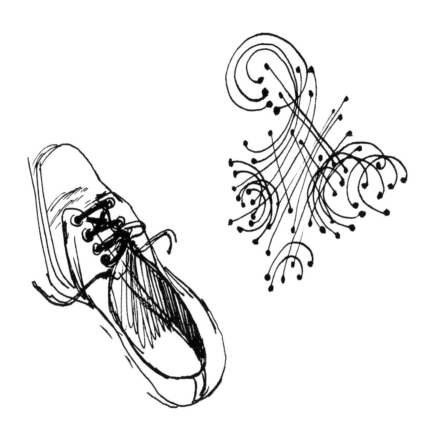

I well remember haystacks; but now, they do not stack hay so much. It goes to baler or grinder. In youth the haystacks rose throughout the hot days, wagonload after wagonload, a boy driver on top feeling the reach of the world; behind him the forks thrust deeply into the load, and to the stacking place where men and wonder waited; skillful stackers could build a symmetrical stack, firm against wind and water, the sides sloping. And when the topping-out was finished and the day's work was over, then in the evening after chores and supper the weary haymakers sometimes crept away and climbed a homemade ladder to the stack's top. There, under stars, with hay odors and the memory of fields and wheels and sun, the boys lay silently looking upward.

Come lie with me

On the stack of new alfalfa

Watch from that

Far elevation

(Pinnacle of boy's wonder)

The dark western line of night-deep clouds

Moving towards us swiftly from far silence

With summer lightning stitching them

And a distant bird calling.

Old rose bushes at the foundation

Of an abandoned homestead,

And what they called backhouse lilies,

Pluming wild down the yard.

I pause here to pluck a cabbage rose,

And wonder if, to some country woman,

The simple roses and the privy lilies

Were her only homestead beauty.